16 EASY PIECES FOR ACCORDION

Free bass accordion

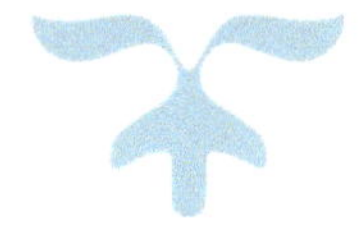

VOL. 1

COSIMO ROSSETTI

Index

Fingering indications for piano accordion and Freebass C System

It is recommended, with regard to registers with 16 ',
to always play the notes written on the staff an octave above.

Aquamarine

Kleiner Tanz

Vals Parisienne

rit.

Windmill Waltz

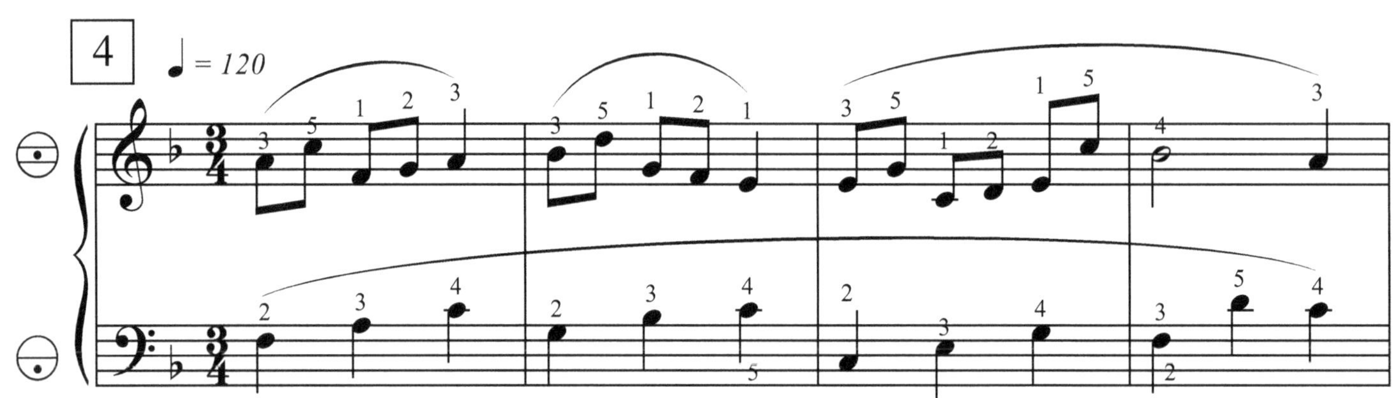

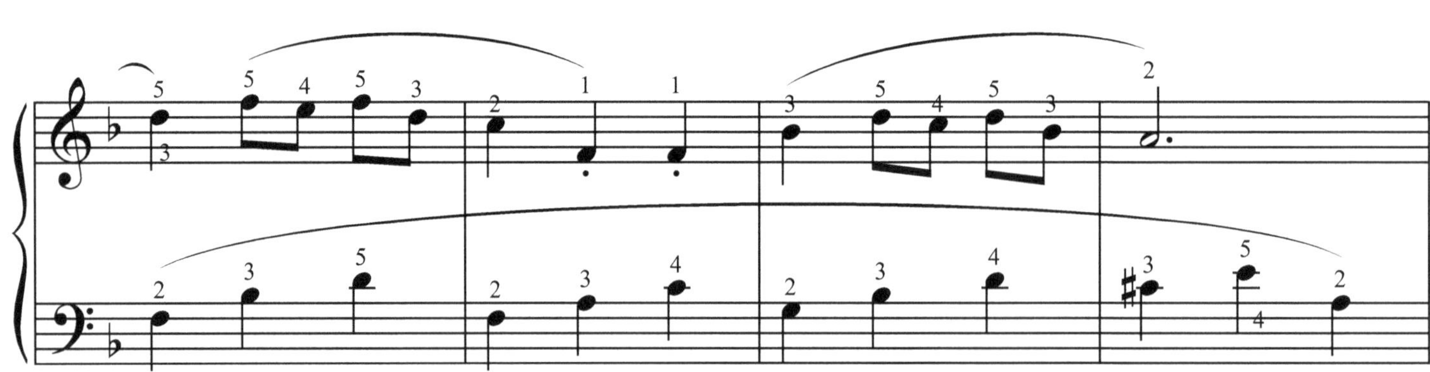

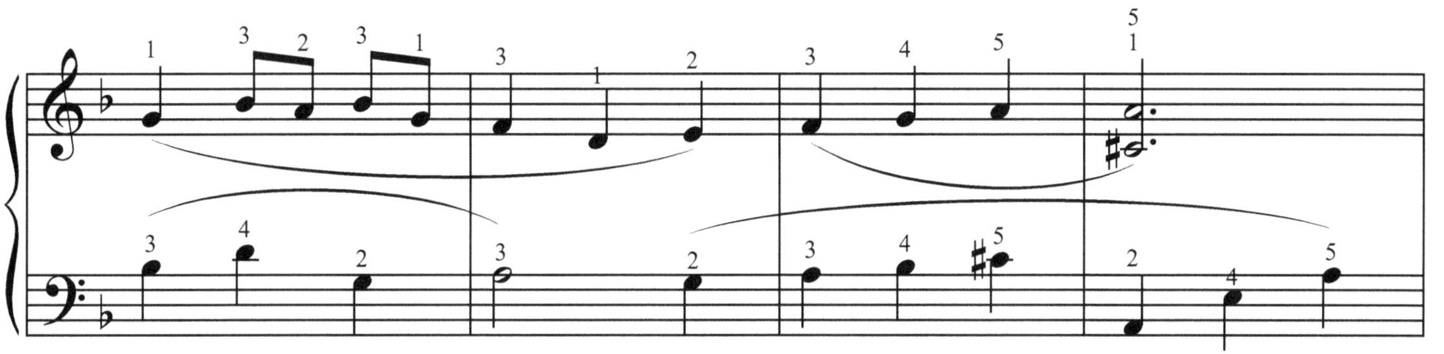

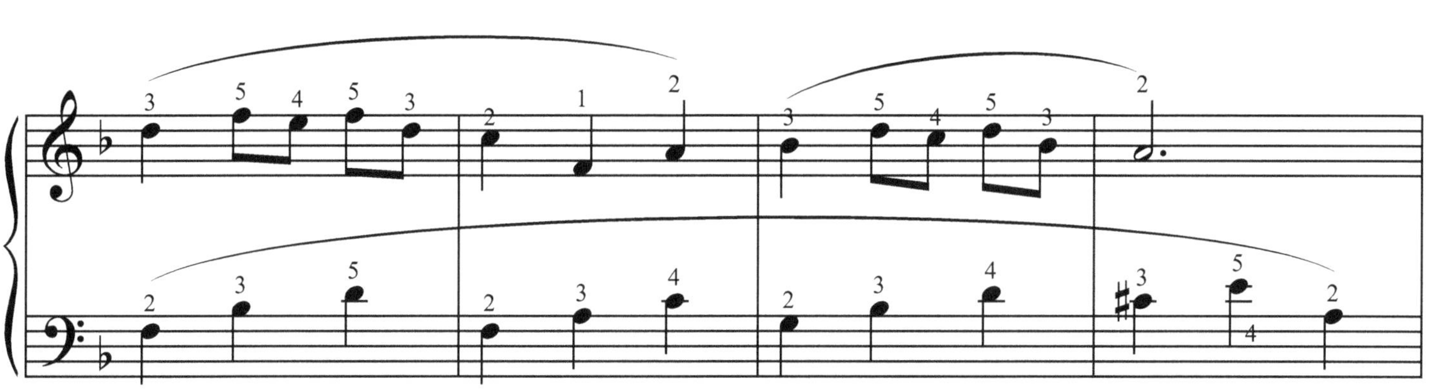

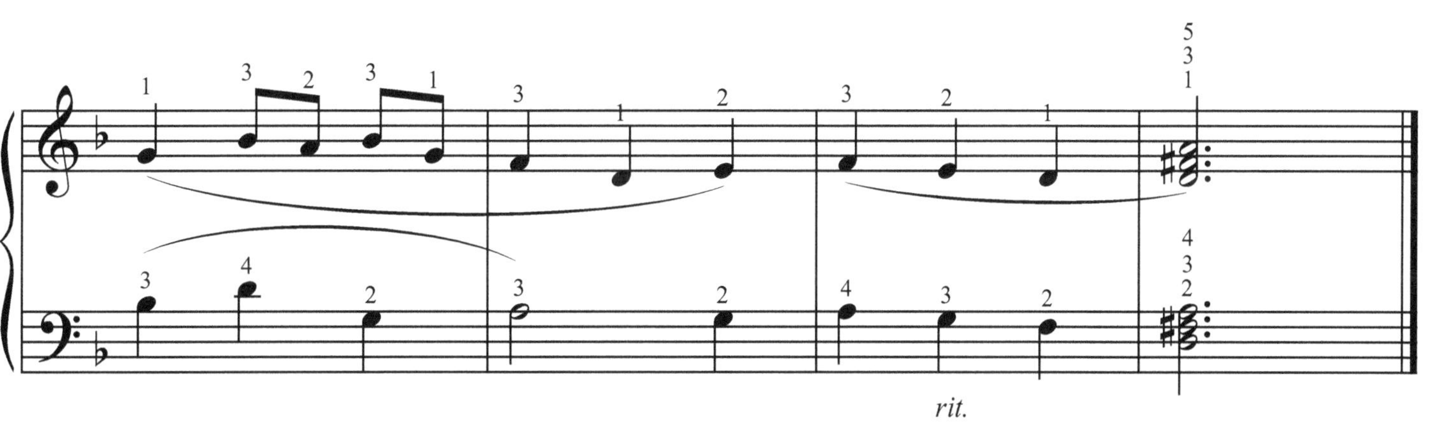

rit.

Sapphire

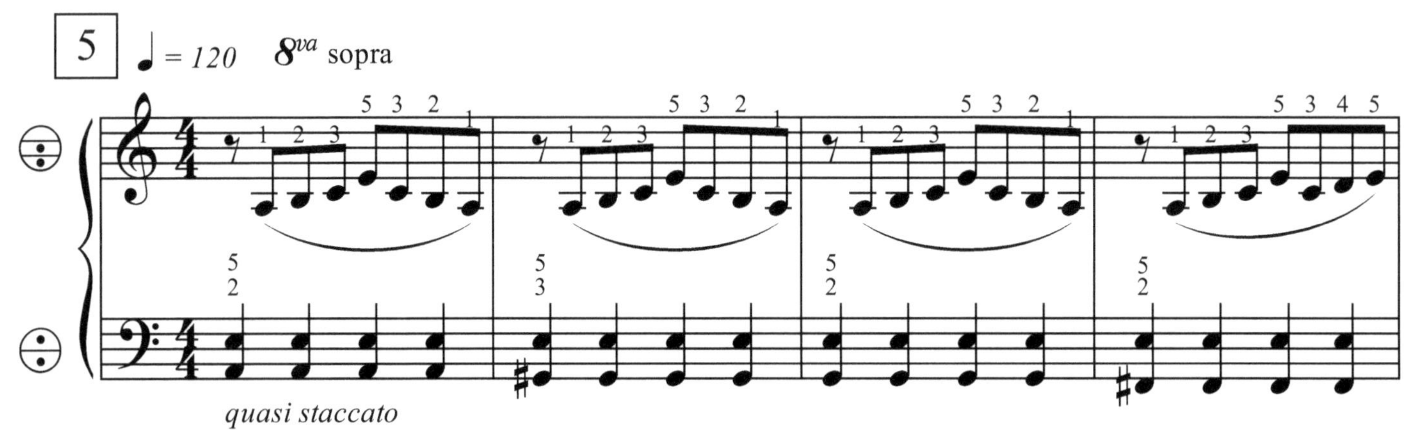

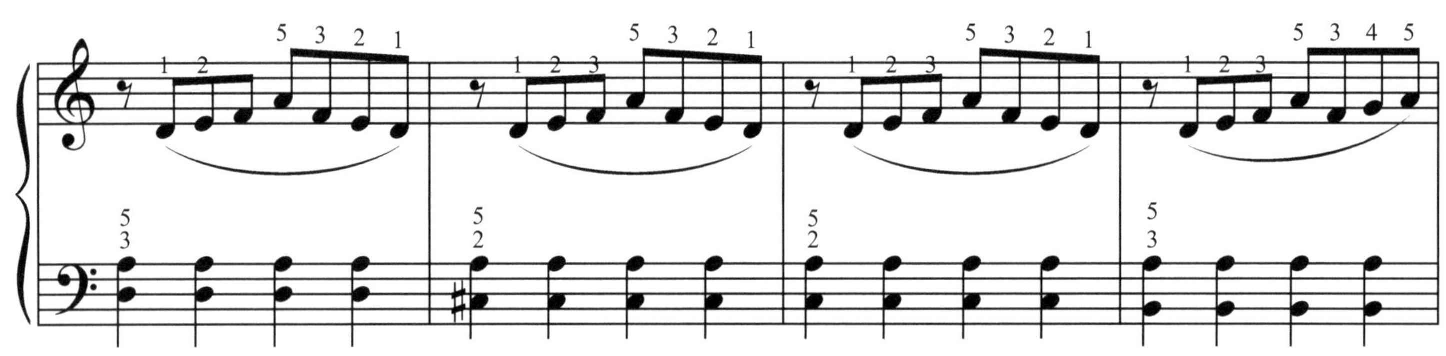

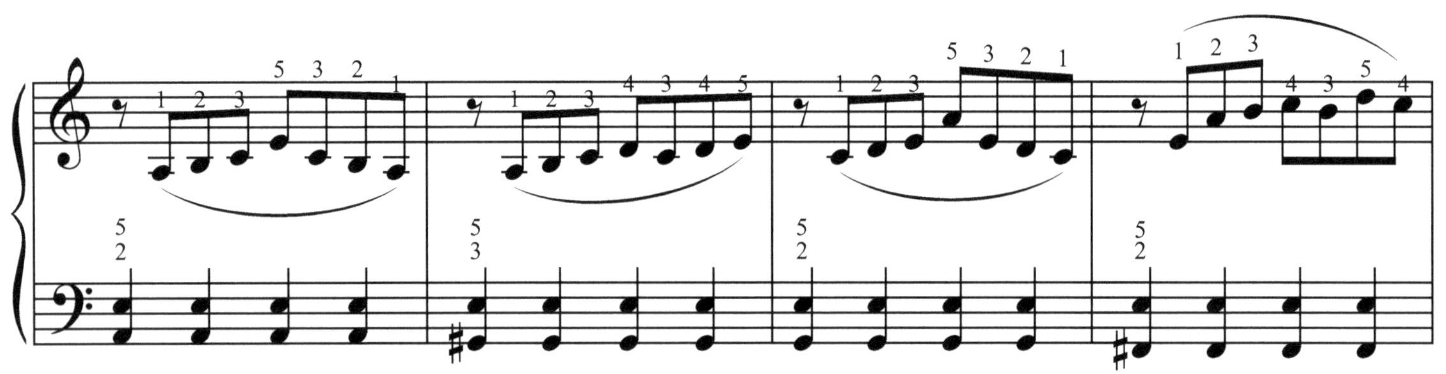

rit.

Ritmo cubano

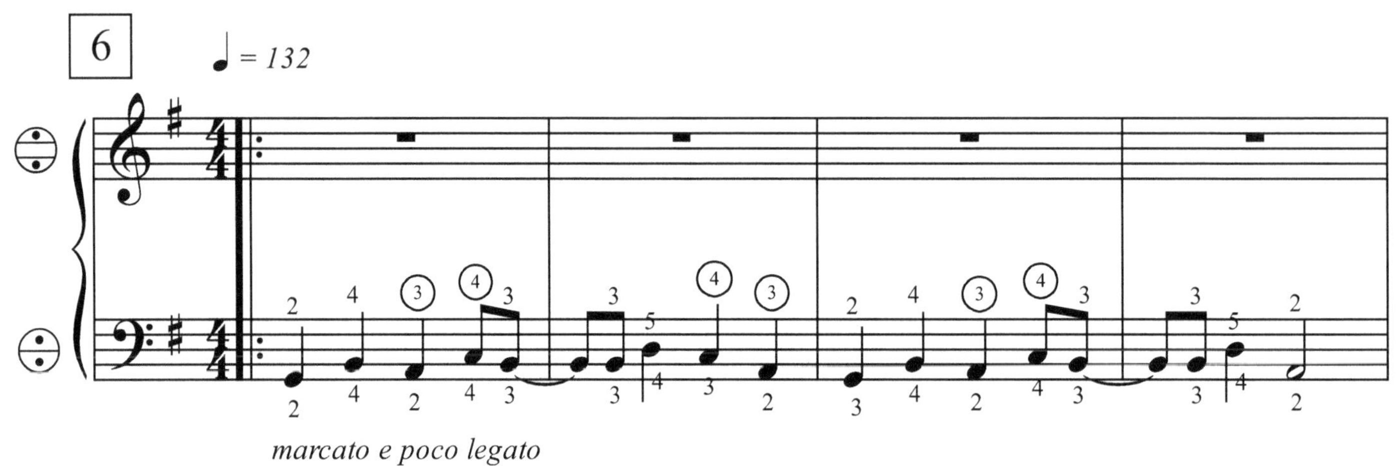

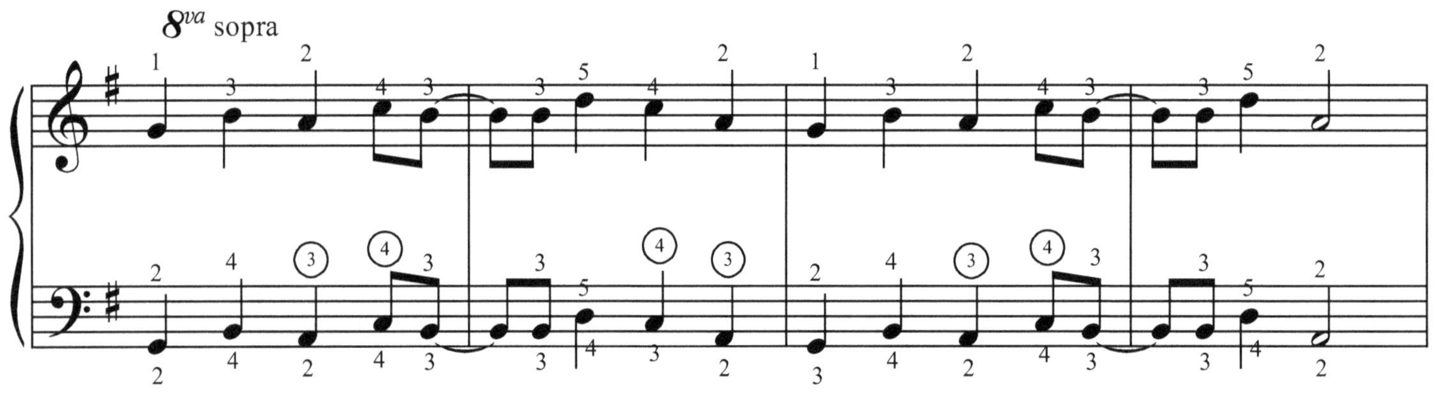

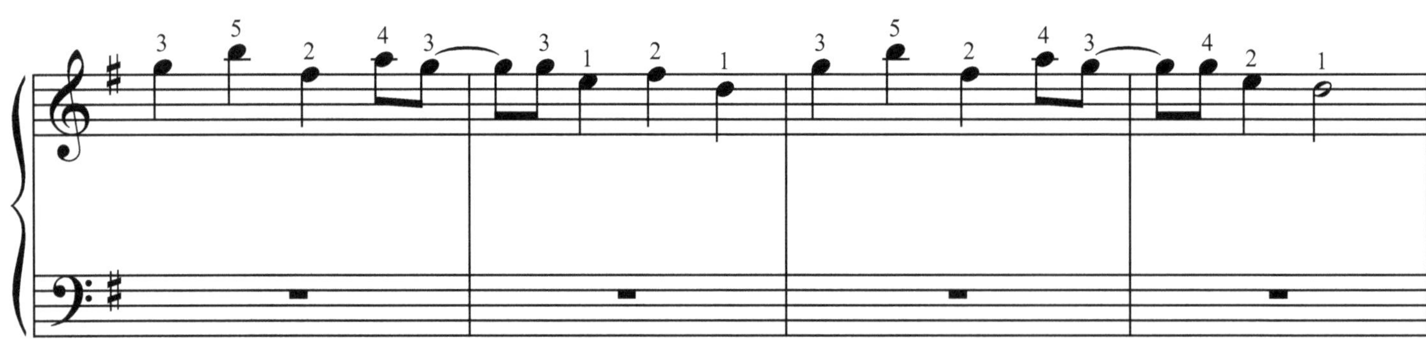

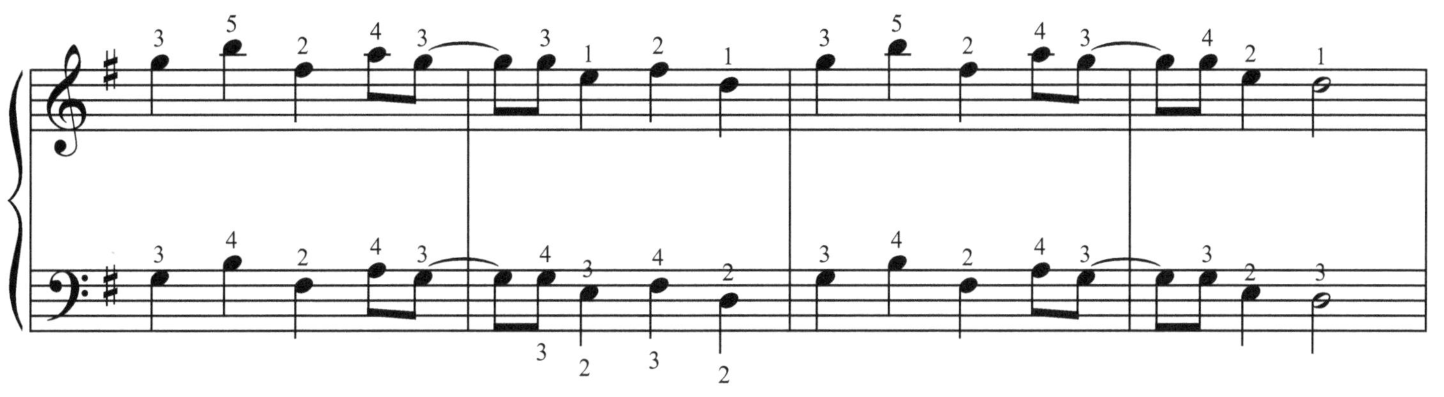

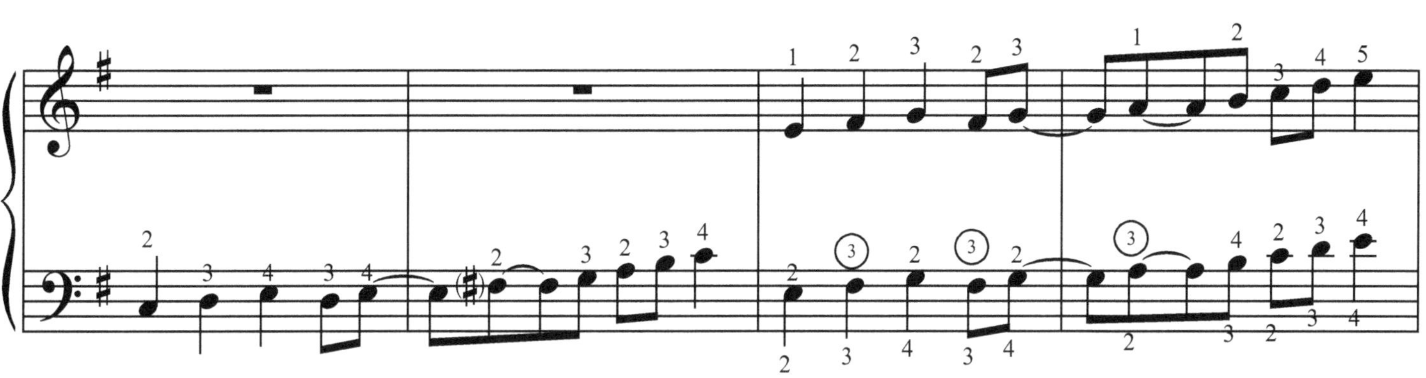

Island

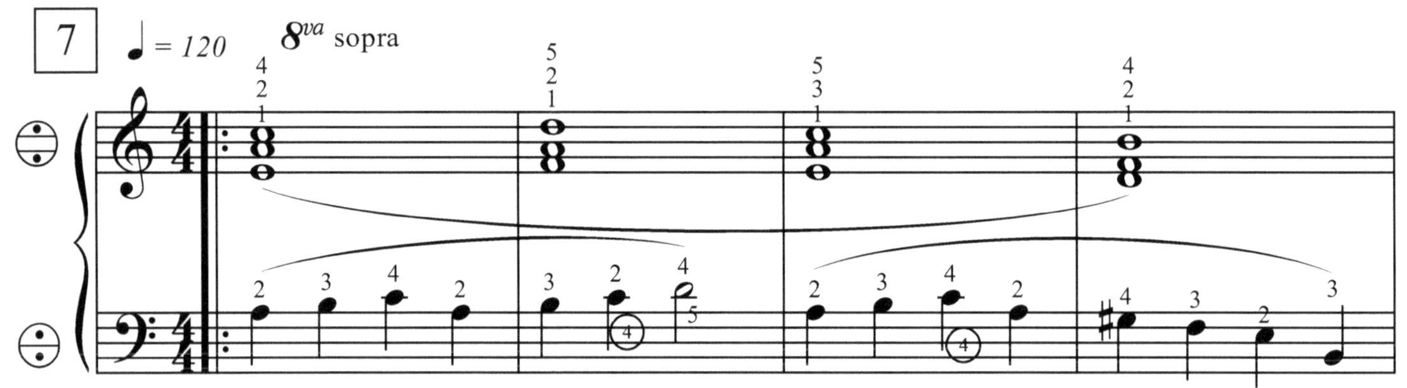

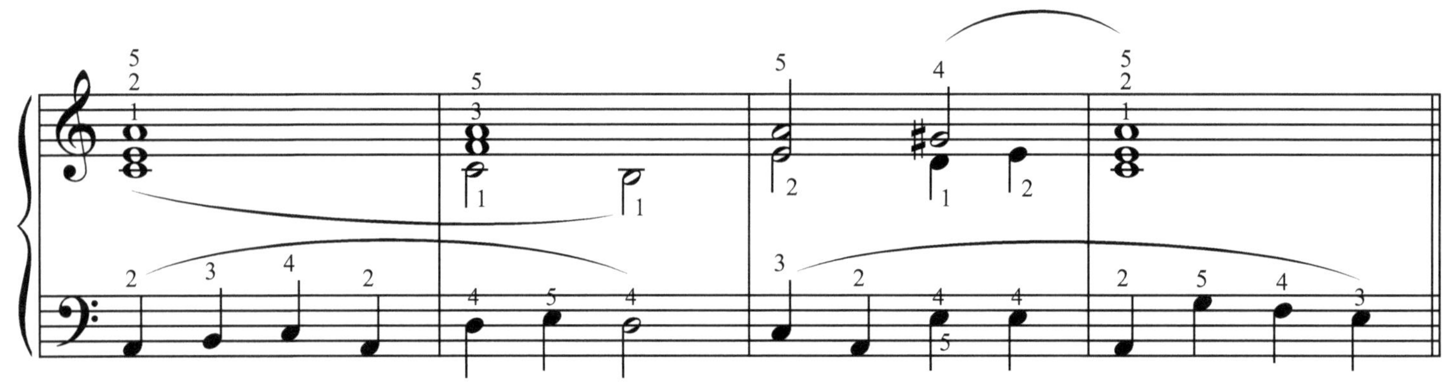

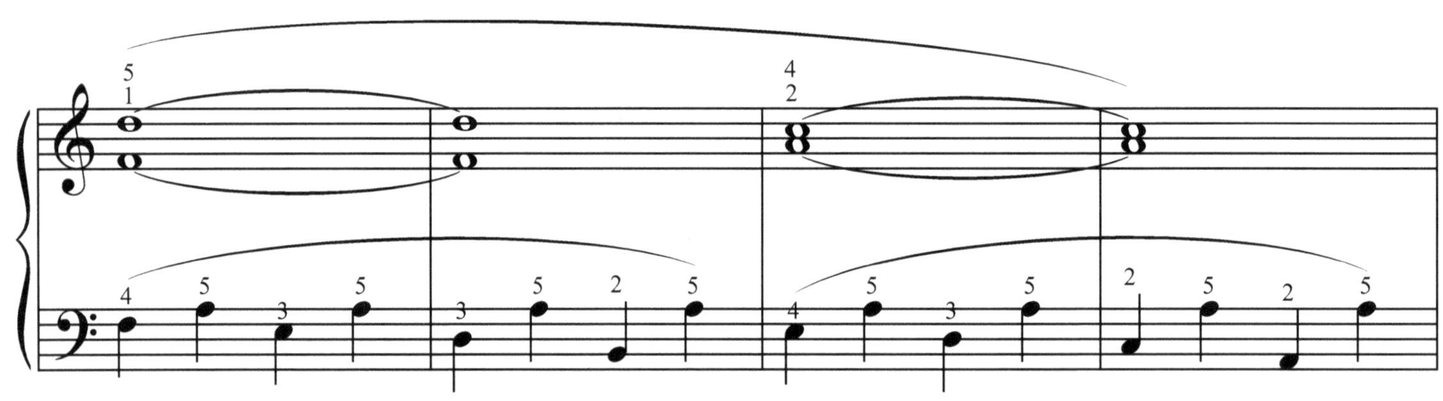

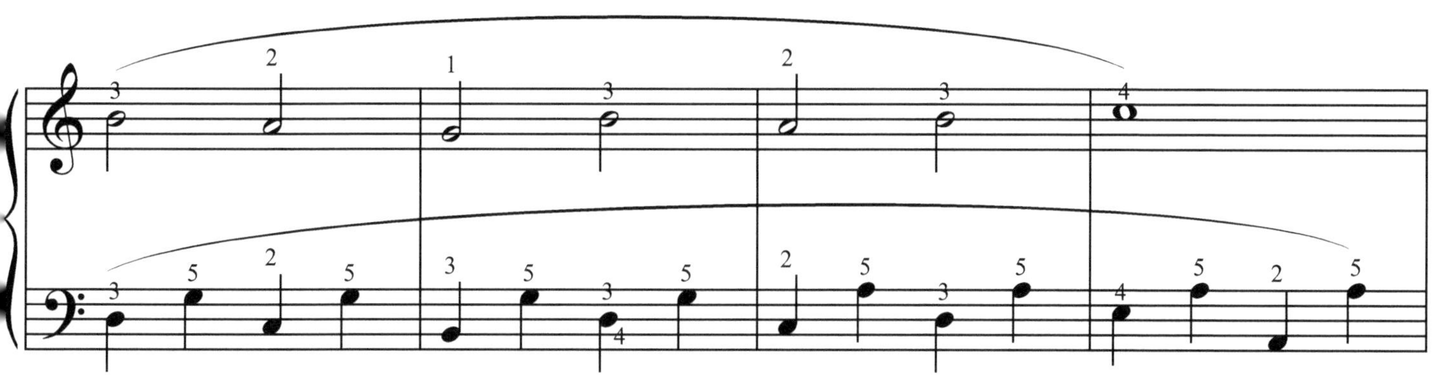

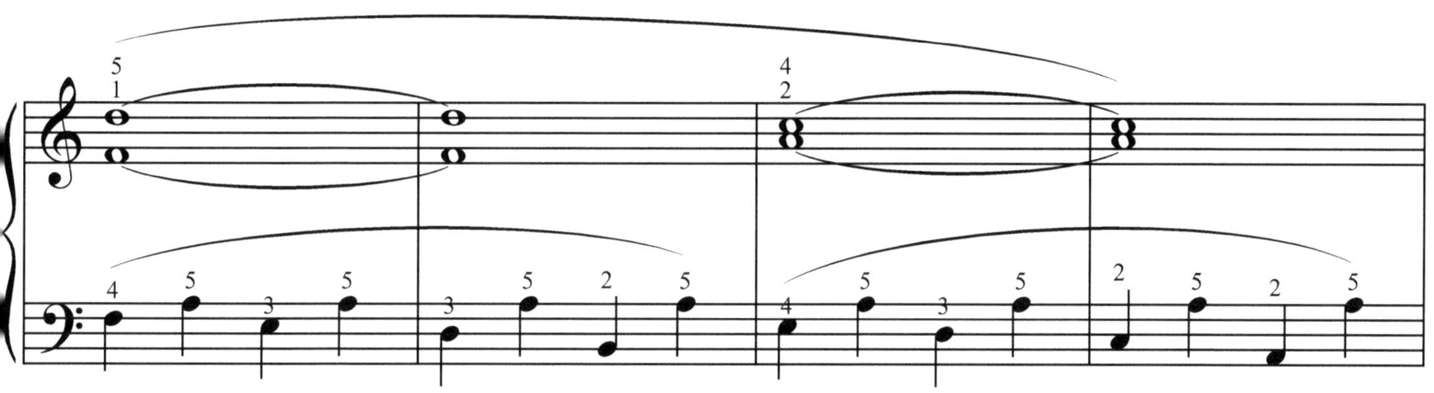

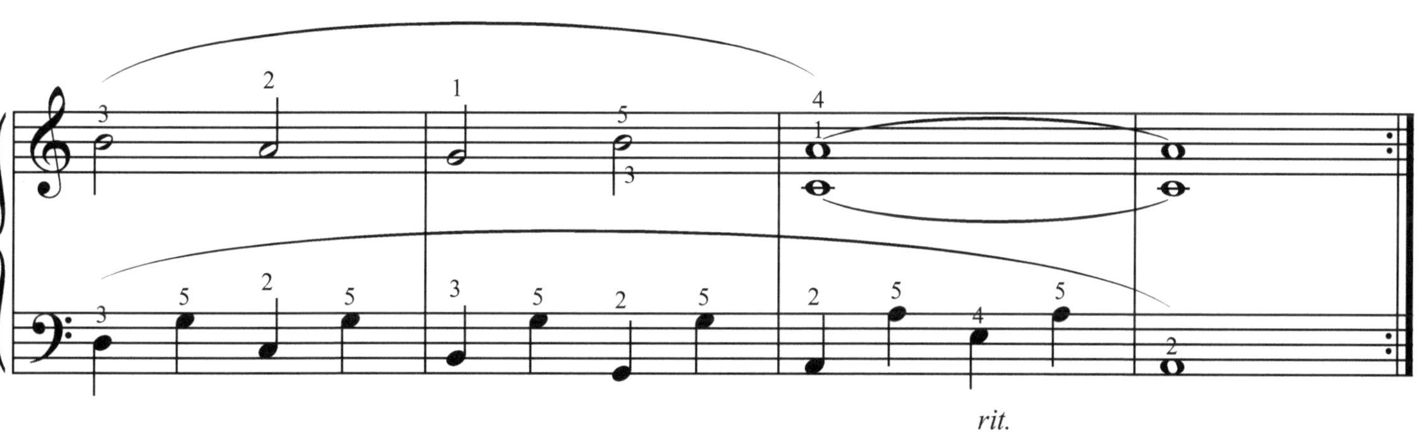
rit.

Österreich

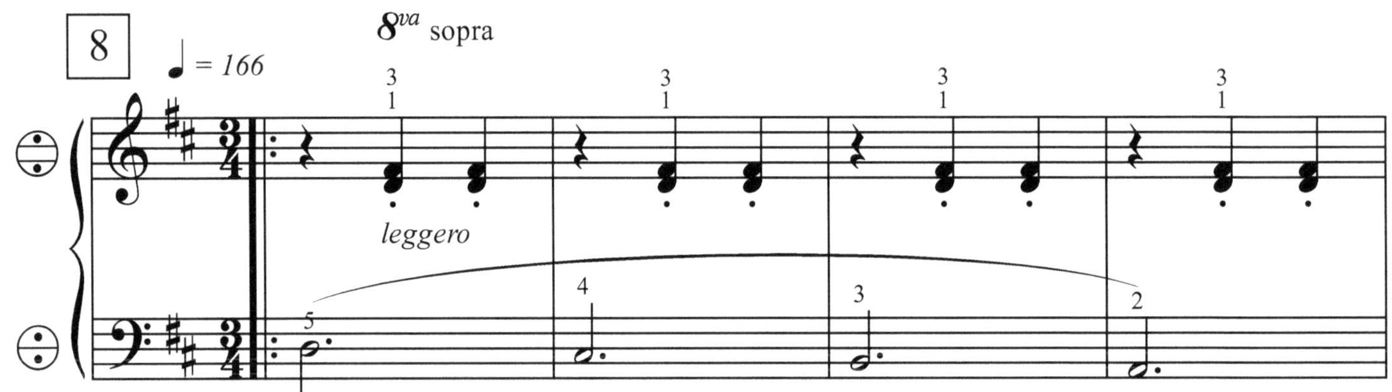

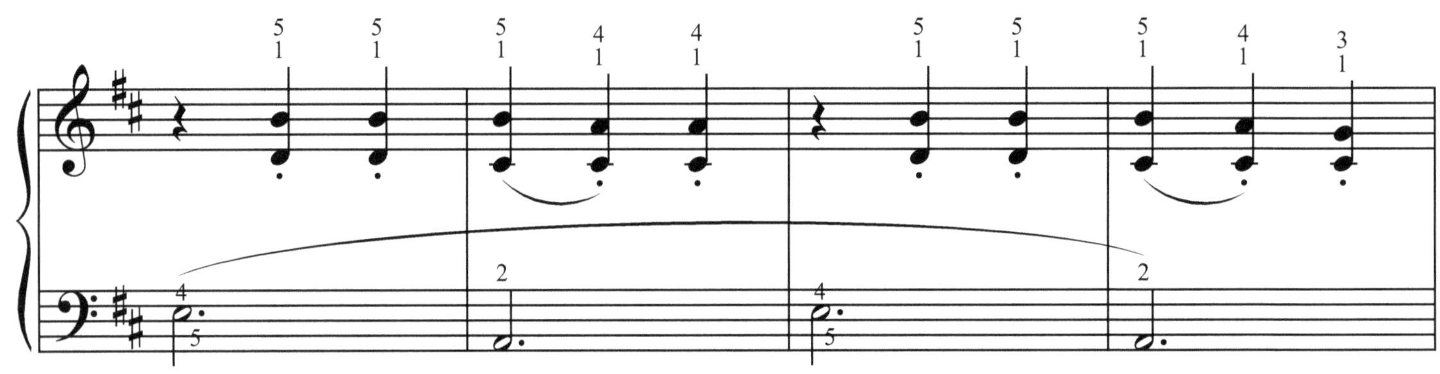

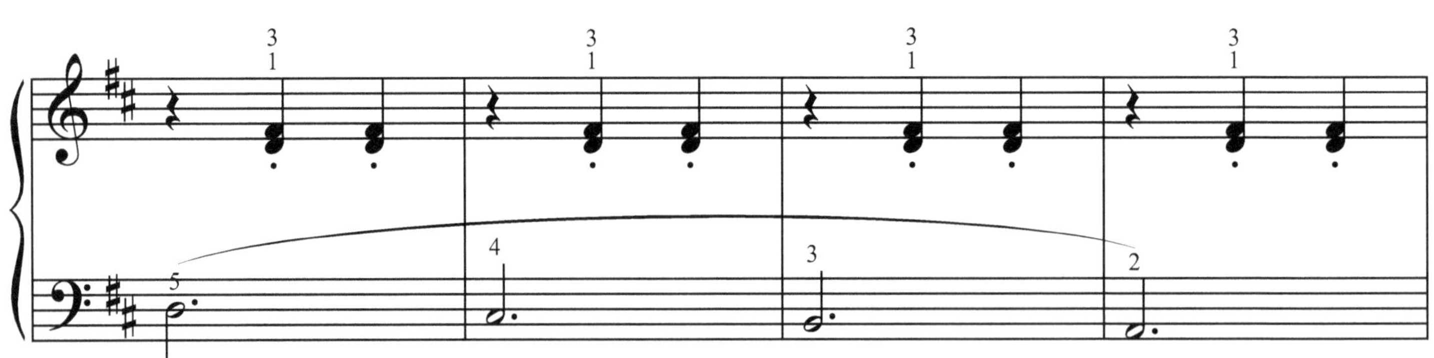

Chase

Alice

Fujiyama

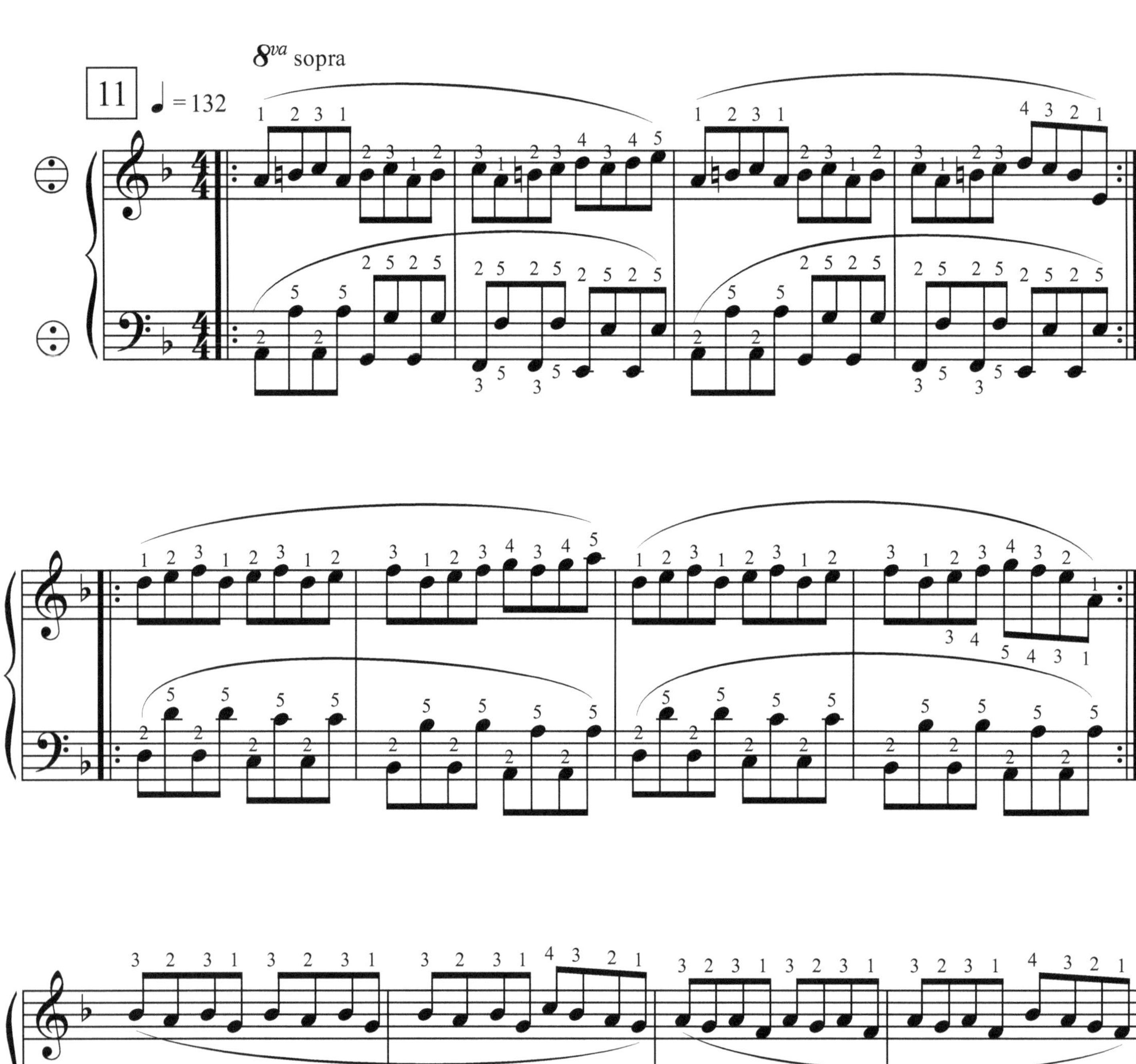

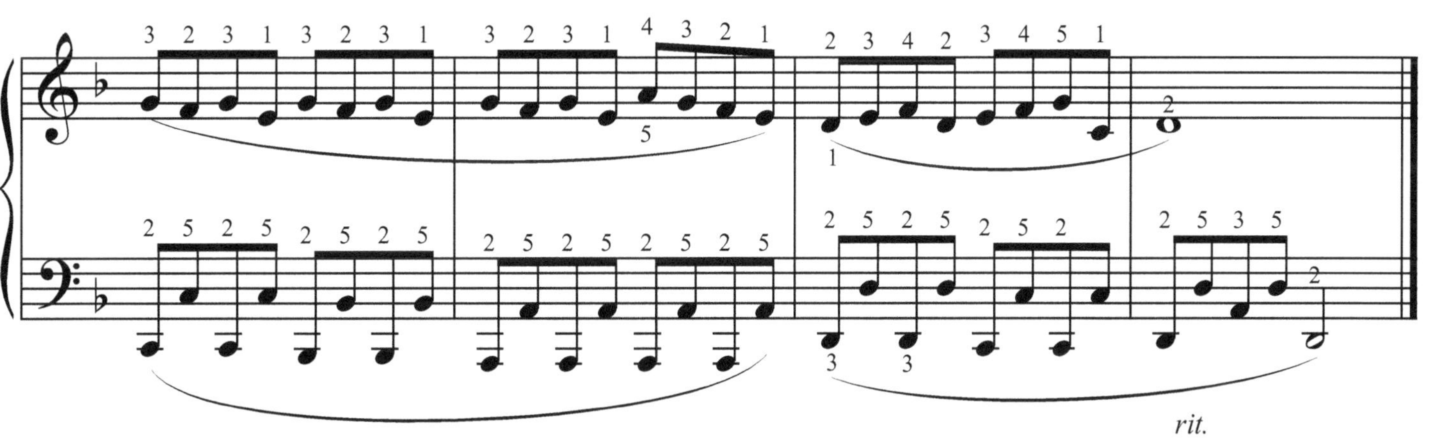
rit.

Elizabeth

8va sopra
rit.

España

rit.

Tango triste

(first version)

Tango triste

(second version)

Tarantella in Am

Eagle